ULTRA COOL RIDES

by
Martin Padgett

Photo credits:

Images courtesy of Martin Padgett

CONTENTS

ULTRA COOL RIDES

Get ready to leave the ordinary four-doors and station wagons behind. The cars in this book are filled with futuristic stylings, earth-shaking horse-power, and all the modern gadgets you can think of (not to mention some you could never imagine). They are the world's fastest, sleekest, and most outrageous vehicles. They are ultra cool rides, all the way.

With cars as awesome as these, who cares about how much cargo room is in back, or how much gas mileage they get? These babies are built for style and speed. How quickly can they shoot from zero to 60 mph? How hot can they look, both inside and out? These cars are head turners, without a doubt.

To top it off, these rides have all been hit with a heavy dose of technology, from ceramic brakes and multivalve engines, to sequential manual gearboxes and space-age aluminum-bonded bodies.

In this book, you'll slip into the seats of cars such as the Ferrari 612 Scaglietti. It's sculpted as beautifully as any Ferrari from the past, but has hammering V-12 power. There's also the new Ford Mustang GT, which combines the best style from all the Mustangs of the past with a thundering 300-horsepower (hp) V-8 engine. Don't forget about the red hot Chevy Corvette, with 400 horsepower, a rear-mounted transmission, a wind-tunnel-tested composite body, and the street and racing creds of a champion. These supercars are mostly about speed and looks, but they're also about what's latest and greatest in the world of ultra cool cars.

CHRYSLER ME 412

Unbelievable. Unimaginable. Unstoppable. All of these words describe the Chrysler ME 412. But don't call it a concept! Chrysler says that this awe-inspiring, quad-turbo V-12 mid-engined supercar is a prototype that will be built and sold to a lucky handful of drivers. If so, it will be the most powerful, fastest American-made supercar. With the help of Germany's AMG, Chrysler took less than a year to build the ME 412, its most advanced vehicle ever.

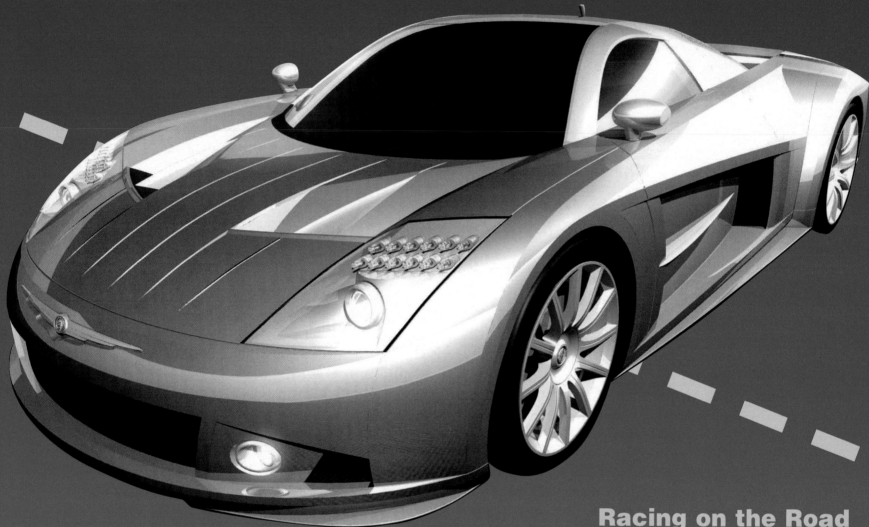

Racing on the Road

The ME 412's body combines carbon-fiber bodywork, aluminum front- and rear-end clips, and metal alloy subframes for the engine and suspension. With racecarlike structural strength, the ME 412 is fitted with lighter suspension, steering, and brake systems that make for world-beating handling and cornering. The brakes, in particular, go beyond the normal supercar standard: They are made of carbon fiber and ceramic, and use six-piston calipers for better stopping capability. Immense 19- and 20-inch cast aluminum wheels wear 265/35ZR19 tires in the front and 335/30ZR20 in the rear. A computer-controlled active rear spoiler comes into play at 186 mph to ensure that the ME 412 sticks to the road at the very top of its range.

Supercar Stats

Supercars need super engines to slingshot them into history. The heart of the ME 412 is its all-aluminum, quad-turbo, 6.0-liter V-12 motor. The ME 412's AMG-developed engine spins out 850 horsepower at a peak of 5,750 rpm. These numbers mean that the ME 412 puts out 142 horsepower per liter of engine displacement—among the best in the world. Plus, it weighs only 2,880 lb, so the ME 412 has a weight-to-power ratio of 3.4 lb/hp—a supercar record.

Chrysler estimates that the ME 412 will hurtle from 0-60 mph in 2.9 seconds, from 0-100 mph in 6.2 seconds, and through the quarter mile in 10.6 seconds at 142 mph. With those numbers, an amazing top speed of 248 mph is within reach!

Super Seating

It isn't enough for a supercar to have a plain interior. The ME 412 makes sure that its cabin is world-class. Chrysler uses the same carbon fiber that is used on the exterior to decorate the dash. Leather-covered sport seats, a tilt steering wheel, automatic climate control, and a premium audio system are fitted into the roomy cockpit. Chrysler promises that the ME 412 will have enough room inside to make drivers forget cramped, foreign exotic cars—especially with a glass roof panel that lets sunshine stream in.

FAST FACTS

Origin:	USA
Top speed:	248 mph
Engine:	quad-turbo-charged 6.0-liter V-12, 850 hp
Length:	178.8 inches
Width:	78.7 inches
Base price:	$350,000 (estimated)

CHEVROLET CORVETTE C6

The Chevrolet Corvette C6, with its sleek and stylish exterior, delivers more power, passion, and precision than any previous 'Vette model. But this new vehicle stays true to its legacy, creating a 21st-century Corvette that both looks to the future and honors the past. The formula from past models remains: extremely high performance capability in a car that also offers great style, quality, and comfort for daily driving. At the same time, "The C6 represents a [major] upgrade to the Corvette," says Dave Hill, Corvette's chief engineer. "We've thoroughly improved performance and developed new features and capabilities in many areas."

Ready to slip into the driver's seat and find out what these fast-riding special features are all about?

Awesome Inner Structure

Chassis is the technical term for the inner structure of a car. The Corvette C6's inside architecture features low weight, high strength, and cored floors. It also is built with an enclosed center tunnel, rear-axle-mounted transmission, and aluminum cockpit. All of these upgraded features enhance the Corvette C6, giving it top speed capability, world-class handling, fantastic fuel efficiency, and a quiet ride inside.

Rev Up the Engine

Under the hood of the C6 is a brand-new LS2 6.0 V-8 engine. This baby raises the bar for standard Corvette performance. It can pump out more than 400 lb-ft of torque (the force that is created between a car's engine and its traction) and can reach a horsepower of 400. It is the largest, most powerful standard small-block engine ever offered in a 'Vette. Not only does the LS2 engine deliver impressive power, it also boasts awesome fuel efficiency. This car packs power, but is also environment-friendly—which is rare in such a hot ride!

Who Needs Keys?

There are no traditional door handles on the C6 Corvette. Instead, the car features keyless access and a push-button start system. This replaces the regular door and hatch mechanics of most cars. (Take a look—do you see a key hole?) The door pops open when remotely activated, and the edge is protected by a small black molding that keeps the finish scratch- and fingerprint-free. In terms of ignition, the push button start system gets this Vette going with—you guessed it—just the push of a button.

An Expressive Face

The Chevy Corvette C6 was designed with character in mind. In the front exposed headlights combine with a center-mounted grille to give the car a distinctive "face." (Can you feel those eyes staring at you?) In the rear, four round taillights feature the Corvette trademark style that dates back to 1961. However, they have been enhanced: When lit, reflector optics give the taillights a glow that looks like the afterburners of a jet. That's one trail-blazing beast!

Radical Wheels

The five-spoke wheels of the C6 are 18 x 8.5 inches at the front and 19 x 10 inches at the rear. They contain extended mobility tires (EMTs) that improve both handling and ride quality. The tires are cutting edge for sure: The design allows them to absorb impact and resist the heat generated by zero-pressure use. They also provide great grip, and roll effortlessly over bumps and potholes, giving lucky drivers an extra smooth—and ultra cool—ride.

Origin:	USA
Top speed:	180.2 mph
Engine:	6.0-liter LS2 V-8, 400 hp
Length:	174.6 inches
Width:	72.6 inches
Base price:	$50,000 (estimated)

LEXUS LF-C

There is no better way for a car company to show off than with a concept car. Concepts let car lovers know what direction a new vehicle will take, and how much it will challenge the competition. The LF-C concept car by Lexus should be causing a stir at BMW headquarters, because it shows that Lexus wants to take on BMW's popular 3-Series in every way possible. As a coupe, as a convertible, and as a high-performance car, it is meant to shoot and scoot with the finest German hardware. It's a preview, in a way, of the next Lexus IS series, and if it's anywhere close to the real thing, look out, BMW. This future-forward car is out of sight!

Four-Way Roof

The LF-C concept shows that Lexus is looking hard at convertibles for its next entry-level car. The LF-C concept sports a four-position retractable hardtop that allows the car to transform itself from a coupe to a convertible at the touch of a button. The powered top stows neatly into the trunk through a small rear-deck opening.

The California-designed LF-C radiates style and speed. Lexus says that the long, integrated lines of the LF-C's body make the shape stand out like no other Lexus before. The roof rail tapers as it moves forward from the rear, making this car look more like a sculpture than like a road rager. Strong and powerful, this concept matches up a futuristic shape with gotta-have-it good looks.

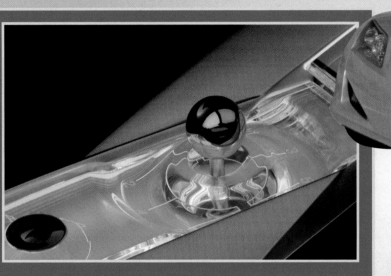

Running the Numbers

Lexus won't give away all the details of the LF-C, but one thing is certain: super speed is a sure thing. That is because the LF-C, in addition to its rear-wheel-drive platform, uses a high-output V-8 engine hooked up to a 6-speed automatic transmission. Lexus doesn't make a V-8 with less than 250 horsepower, so it looks like the sky is the limit for the LF-C. Then there are the massive tires: 20-inchers in the front, 21-inchers in the rear—more than enough grip for this 4-passenger concept. All in all, this supercar won't quit, and its space-age looks make it out of this world!

Blue-Light Special

The cockpit of the LF-C is a mixture of race-carlike mechanicals and iMac-inspired details. It has drive-by-wire steering, which means that computers tell the engine and transmission how to work together. A velour-coated steering wheel is complemented by gauges stacked on top of the steering column. The center console runs between the front and rear seats. The displays and controls are hidden beneath the console's transparent surface, and soft blue lighting glows from beneath. Four individual bucket seats are slim and trim, to emphasize the LF-C's futuristic theme.

Origin:	Japan
Top speed:	150 mph
Engine:	V-8
Length:	178.7 inches
Width:	73.0 inches
Base price:	$35,000 (estimated)

MAZDA IBUKI

The name *Ibuki* comes from a Japanese word meaning "breathing new energy into." This is certainly true of the Mazda Ibuki concept, which, out of all the gas/electric hybrids trying to be sports cars on the show floor, has the best shot at production. Why? Because it is a lightweight roadster with a lively personality. Plus, it adds a self-regenerating electric motor and an automatic engine-shut-off feature (to reduce fuel consumption at idle). Since it doesn't weigh much to begin with, the eye-catching Ibuki doesn't need tremendous amounts of power to be worthy as a sports car. Its look alone makes it ultra cool!

Lightweight, Fun, and Fabulous

"The aim of this concept was to further refine the fun-to-drive spirit that [can come] from a lightweight, convertible sports car," says Truman Pollard, chief designer of Mazda North American Operations. The Ibuki is built with lightweight materials, such as reinforced plastic for the fenders, rear floor panels, and outer door panels. The propeller shaft and power-plant frame are made of carbon fiber, while the wheels are of magnesium alloy. These featherlight materials keeps the overall vehicle weight low. Short front and rear overhangs yield a trim roadster that's over 12 inches shorter than the current Miata, which is pretty small and lightweight itself!

Safety First!

Mazda has spared no expense when it comes to the safety features of this concept car. The protective front end provides a good crushable zone in the event of a collision. The 18-inch wheels are made of magnesium alloy, and they're fitted with run-flat tires. The Ibuki incorporates a sensor that would activate a four-point rollover bar in the event of a rollover under impact. The active roll bar would instantly lift up via sensors, saving the day—and anyone inside.

Inside/Outside

The Ibuki's interior is as slick and sleek as its exterior. The air-conditioning system is placed behind the seats, so the engine can be mounted much farther to the rear. Spot-cooling zones provide cool air during summer, while a heating zone traps warm air inside to ensure it is comfortable in the cabin during open-top driving, even on the coldest of days. In addition, a new audio system, which combines the seat air-conditioning ducts and speaker in one unit, delivers much clearer sounds. And guess what's even cooler? A keyless entry ID card that can be used by the lucky driver.

Efficient Engine

The Mazda Ibuki is powered by a lightweight and compact 16-valve MZR 1.6-liter, inline, 4-cylinder engine. It features an integrated electric hybrid motor which, at low engine speeds, provides torque assistance to boost acceleration from a standing start. To save fuel and reduce emissions, the hybrid motor automatically stops the engine from idling when the car is still. The motor then restarts the engine automatically when the driver steps on the gas pedal. But there's more: During deceleration, the hybrid motor functions as a generator, recharging the car's battery. The Ibuki also features a 6-speed manual transmission. The transmission weighs less than the gearbox of the current MX-5 Miata, and is fitted with synchronizers that make shifting feel decisive, yet smooth.

FAST FACTS

Origin:	Japan
Top speed:	Not yet determined
Engine:	1.6-liter, 180 hp
Length:	143.3 inches
Width:	67.7 inches
Base price:	$20,000 (estimated)

JAGUAR XK-RS

This hot ride is the Jaguar XK-RS concept convertible. It's an extreme makeover of Jaguar's XKR roadster. The XK-RS boosts power, increases the sleek ragtop's width, and puts a serious punch into its potential price tag. It isn't easy to turn a street-riding roadster into a thundering 200-mph supercar, but if it's power that drivers want, they'll find it here, in one of the world's best-looking convertibles. It is the most powerful road-going Jaguar convertible ever. This cat has got all the claws a driver will need to shred some serious pavement.

Looks Like a Winner!

Inside and out, the XK-RS looks every bit the supercar it's been transformed into. This concept is painted a deep, lustrous black lacquer with leaping-cat decals on the car's sides, like those on Jaguar's race cars.

This Jaguar's cockpit is a mixture of modern and classic styles. The XK's DVD navigation system is located right on the steering wheel. Gorgeous wood on the dash, real wood and chrome trim covering the console, and a super high-power audio system with 10 speakers makes this one radical ride.

Dynamic Results

Stuffing a massively powerful engine under the hood of a supercar isn't all a car needs to become a legend. That is why Jaguar's engineers worked on the XK-RS's suspension and body to make sure that the handling was up to the 550-horsepower challenge. For one, they took a look at the underside of the car to improve the way the air flows beneath the car. The smoother the airflow, the more stable a car is at higher speeds. In the end, they created special under-body air tunnels that run the length of the car, along with deeper front and rear spoilers, and wider wheel arches like those used on the specially-developed XKR that starred in the James Bond flick *Die Another Day*.

To top it all off, the XK-RS comes fitted with 3-piece wheels—center-lock Machiavelli Gotti wheels, 20-inch x 10-inch at the front, 20-inch x 11-inch at the rear—shod with high-performance Michelin Pilot tires. This makes for smooth sailing all the way.

Powering Up

How did Jaguar turn its XKR roadster into this XK-RS supercar? For starters, Jaguar took the already-potent Jaguar V-8 engine and boosted its displacement to 5.0 liters, then strapped on an Eaton charger for a serious power infusion. It also installed new valves, new stainless-steel exhaust headers, a new fuel-injection system, and other go-fast pieces. The results are awesome: This Jag spits out an estimated 550 horsepower and 500 lb-ft of torque, which makers say will slingshot the car from 0-60 mph in fewer than four seconds. This will take the XK-RS to a top speed of 200 mph. The stock 6-speed ZF automatic transmission has been exchanged for a heavy-duty 5-speed manual gearbox to give it that speed capability. This also shifts some of the car's weight to the back end, for better balance and handling.

Origin:	Great Britain
Top speed:	186 mph
Engine:	6.0-liter V-12, 450 hp
Length:	187.4 inches
Width:	75.0 inches
Base price:	$125,000 (estimated)

AUDI LE MANS QUATTRO

Audi is known around the world for its all-wheel-drive racing and rally cars. So it's no surprise that the hottest concept ever to come from this German car company would be an all-wheel-drive supercar. The Le Mans Quattro concept won the Le Mans 24-hour race 3 times. Behind its awesome looks lies awesome supercar power, thanks to Audi's first-ever V-10 engine. It's a sizzling concept car sure to be built for the road—and sure to be the hottest supercar ever to come from Germany!

Open It Up

The Le Mans Quattro has more technology than you can imagine crammed into its slingshot shape. The car's frame creates a super-strong body from which the car's panels are hung. The panels are made of a blend of aluminum and carbon fiber, which makes the body super light and super strong. Double-wishbone suspension at the front and rear is set for sportscar handling and, teamed with Audi's magnetic shock absorbers, it makes for an easy ride.

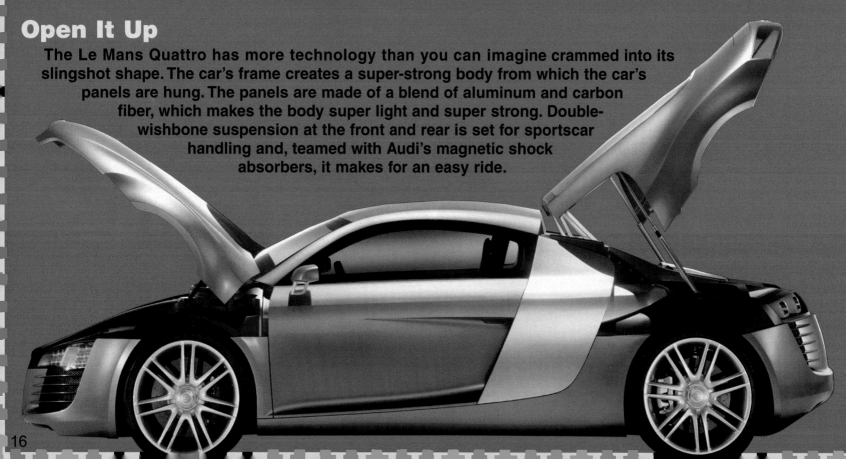

Nose to Nose

The Le Mans Quattro looks like pure speed, with its jet-blue paint job and its tight, athletic stance. The bullish front end makes the car look like it's getting ready for a 500-yard sprint. In between, the roofline soars like the canopy of a fighter jet. Wide but short, the Le Mans's body is like a speeding bullet. The exterior sports a classic Audi grille and LED headlights. Massive air intakes and outlets feed the V-10 engine, brakes, oil cooler, and turbos. The rock-solid wheels with flared arches stand out, big and bold.

Earth-Shaking Engine

The major earthshaker under this car's rear panels is Audi's first V-10 engine—a 5.0-liter, twin-turbocharged motor with direct fuel injection. It has been placed mid-engine and arranged longitudinally—from nose to tail—for better power transfer. The engine makes constant torque of more than 600 lb-ft from 1,750 rpm to 5,800 rpm. Audi designed this motor to make it free-revving, and mated it to a 6-speed manual gearbox to use all the power at hand.

Like most other Audis, the Le Mans Quattro concept sports permanent all-wheel drive. The system doesn't just put the power to the rear—it decides which wheels need the most power and delivers it instantly for the best driving. Audi makers think that this combination of engine, gearbox, and all-wheel drive will let the Le Mans steam to 60 mph in fewer than 3.7 seconds, and to 125 mph in 10.8 seconds. Now that's ultra cool—and ultra fast!

First-Class Cabin

The Le Mans Quattro's cockpit is built for speed. It features large gauges, a custom-shaped steering wheel, and a driving position created specifically for high-speed maneuvers. But Audi made sure that, unlike other supercars, the Le Mans Quattro isn't useful only on the track: The interior is large enough for two, with the high-quality materials and cozy comfort that make this cabin a first-class ride.

FAST FACTS	
Origin:	Germany
Top speed:	186 mph
Engine:	5.0-liter twin-turbo V-10, 610 hp
Length:	172.0 inches
Width:	74.8 inches
Base price:	$150,000 (estimated)

HUMMER H2 SUT

The only vehicle on the road that has seen military action in a generation is the Humvee, and GM's Hummer H2 is descended from that tough military SUV's body. But the H2 doesn't just come as a pure SUV anymore. The Hummer brand is turning the idea of a flexible off-roader one notch higher with the H2 SUT (sports-utility truck)—a vehicle with unmatched capabilities, and still every inch a Hummer. Like the H2 SUV, the SUT has unbelievable off-road capability. Also like the SUV, this SUT can carry passengers, cargo, or a combination of the two, and can haul like any other open-bed pickup. It's the ultimate off-road vehicle for four people who need to carry a lot of gear outside the cabin.

Rugged Ranger

The H2 SUT's exterior is as rugged as its interior is refined. The Hummer's heritage can be seen in the flat, chiseled sheetmetal; the hard body lines; and the flat glass panes. These features not only make for better interior room and give the H2 better visibility, they also directly relate the SUT to military vehicles. The same is true for some of the H2 SUT's hardware. Its hood-lift handles, hood latches, and fasteners give this vehicle a cool Tonkalike look, as if the driver could take it apart if needed.

Off-road details make the difference between the Hummer SUT and less capable off-roaders. The rear bumper sports large, military, Hummer-style retrieval loops. The front bumper includes tow loops. Both bumpers have access holes for the hitch receivers attached to the chassis. These access holes can accommodate a winch, which is a device made to help pull out other vehicles that get stuck in off-road muck. Both receivers accommodate a regular Class 3 trailer hitch, a necessity for towing such heavy off-road toys as boats and Jet Skis.

When it comes to pure off-road driving, the H2 SUT has the goods to get you there. Short overhangs, front and back, ensure that the driver won't crunch the body on steep rocks, and exceptional ground clearance means a smoother ride on bumpy trails. The 17-inch wheels, heavy-duty independent front suspension, and 5-link rear suspension provide superior handling, and carrying and towing capability.

The engine stuffed under this Hummer's hood gives it unequaled on- and off-road power. A version of GM's 6.0-liter, Vortec 6000 V-8, it delivers 325 horsepower at 5,200 rpm and 365 lb-ft of torque at 4,000 rpm. The Vortec 6,000 is mated to a heavy-duty Hydra-Matic 4-speed automatic overdrive transmission, with full-time all-wheel drive. Basically, there is no stopping this baby!

Tough, But Totally Luxurious

The H2 SUT's interior features power leather seats in tan or black. There is no shortage of electronics inside, either. When a driver is far off the beaten path, the H2 SUT's touch-screen navigation radio can help the driver find the way back. With the push of a button, the navigation operation will instantly map routes with 2-D and 3-D full-color map views on a 5.8-inch display screen, making maneuvering on highways and streets effortless. OnStar, the safety and entertainment communication system from GM, is standard, and XM satellite radio is an option.

FAST FACTS

Origin:	USA
Top speed:	125 mph
Engine:	6.0-liter V-8, 325 hp
Length:	189.8 inches
Width:	81.2 inches
Base price:	$50,000

SUBARU WRX STi

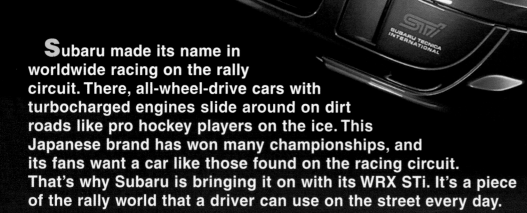

Subaru made its name in worldwide racing on the rally circuit. There, all-wheel-drive cars with turbocharged engines slide around on dirt roads like pro hockey players on the ice. This Japanese brand has won many championships, and its fans want a car like those found on the racing circuit. That's why Subaru is bringing it on with its WRX STi. It's a piece of the rally world that a driver can use on the street every day.

Stirring Up Power

The 2.5-liter four-cylinder engine in the WRX STi starts life as a mild-mannered 165-horsepower motor. By the time it gets electronic throttle control, turbocharging and intercooling, forged pistons (for strength and high-speed durability), and variable valve timing for more precise fuel delivery, this engine is transformed into a 300-horsepower beast that shrieks out its power. The engine is coupled with a close-ratio, 6-speed manual transmission that uses double-cone synchronizers on first, third, and reverse gears, with a triple-cone on second. It also has an internal oil pump to ensure that the transmission can handle the Subaru's immense power.

Racing Beat

The style of the plain-Jane WRX gets jacked up into racer heaven through lots of body tweaks. The STi wears a bigger hood scoop than the regular WRX, one that is functional, too: The hood feeds more air to a bigger intercooler. The headlights are set up with five different lights inside, as well as smoke-tinted lenses. The driver can aim the headlights from a control knob inside the cockpit. The back windshield is made of superlight glass, and there's no standard sound system— all to inforce this car's let's-go-racing attitude. Every STi gets the same interior, with blue floor mats and seats, and performance-minded front buckets with blue bolsters. The gray leather steering wheel has rockin' red stitching.

Hardware for Hard Driving

Along with the engine and gearbox, the STi gets some no-holds-barred hardware that gives it great all-weather handling on top of scorching power. The all-wheel drive sports a driver control center differential, which allows the driver to select how much power goes to the front and rear wheels. The steering gear is tighter, for a more precise feeling. The suspension has aluminum components that cut down on the weight sitting on the wheels, which improves the car's responses. The huge 4-wheel disk brakes, 12.7 inches up front and 12.3-inches in back, have antilock control. Clearly, this car has what it takes to handle ultra hard driving.

FAST FACTS

Origin:	Japan
Top speed:	150 mph
Engine:	2.5-liter turbocharged flat four, 300 hp
Length:	173.8 inches
Width:	68.5 inches
Base price:	$31,445

FERRARI 612 SCAGLIETTI

A new Ferrari 2+2 (a car with two full seats up front and two smaller seats in back) comes around only a few times in a lifetime. The new 612 Scaglietti could be the most breathtaking, most beautiful Ferrari in generations. This sleek coupe is named in honor of Sergio Scaglietti, one of the company's first coach builders and a master at sculpting aluminum panels. This four-seater honors his memory with a stunning shape that takes details from Ferraris of the past and blends them with a striking stance; a broad, curvy body; and ultra cool technology never before seen in Italy's 2+2 coupes. It's the ultimate Ferrari for four, and a driver's dream—for only a quarter-million dollars!

Fire Under the Hood

The centerpiece of any Ferrari road car is its engine. In the 612 Scaglietti, the engine is a fantastic-sounding, deep-growling, horsepower-howling V-12. It's a new, all-aluminum, 48-valve, 5.75-liter V-12 with drive-by-wire controls, which means that computers are used between driver and engine to gauge throttle inputs. The engine churns out 532 horsepower—98 horses more than previous models—and twists out 434 lb-ft of torque. Ferrari says that the Scaglietti will scoot from 0-60 mph in 4.1 seconds, about a tenth of a second faster than older 2+2s. Top speed, says Ferrari, is an unreal 196 mph. The engine fires up its amazing power through a choice of a six-speed manual transmission or a new 6-speed, electrohydraulic semiautomatic. The gearbox uses paddles mounted behind the steering wheel to push shifts up and down—without the driver having to take his or her hands off the steering wheel.

Tons of Technology

Ferraris are among the best-engineered cars on the planet, but the Italian carmakers usually leave off most of the electronics when it comes to their cars' performance. The 612 Scaglietti breaks that mold to make its supercar performance more usable for everyday drivers. The 612 sports the company's first use of stability control, which uses a car's antilock brake sensors to predict when it is losing grip, then to correct the situation with braking power. The 612 also gets traction control and antilock brakes, to ensure the safety of the driver and three passengers. Speed-sensitive power steering is included, too, as well as dual front airbags; dual-zone digital climate control; power seats, windows and doors; automatic rain-sensing wipers; and a Bose premium audio system with a trunk-mounted six-disk CD changer.

Bold Body

The cool curves and irresistible proportions of the 612 Scaglietti prove that beauty isn't just skin deep. This Ferrari's stunning shape is created atop an aluminum space frame and body. Compared to the 456M (the previous Ferrari to seat four), it has a more solid structure. As a result of the stiffer body, Ferrari was able to shift the powertrain back and down within the body for better weight distribution. This helps the new Ferrari handle better. The stronger body even allowed engineers to create a bigger cabin without sacrificing performance. Even the trunk is about 25 percent larger than the former Ferrari model.

Origin:	Italy
Top speed:	186 mph
Engine:	5.75-liter V-12, 532 hp
Length:	192.9 inches
Width:	77.0 inches
Base price:	$250,000

MASERATI MC12

The Maserati MC12 is a dynamic—and dynamite—car. Designed for high-level road use, it can go from 0 to 60 in just 3.7 seconds. At full throttle, this ride can reach a top speed of 205.1 mph. About 30 MC12s are scheduled to be built, 25 of which will be sold for road use. The 25 cars will be available only in the blue and white design. The remaining 5 will be built only for show, and will sport a hot paint job that screams Maserati. Chances are, you'll never see one of these babies in real life. This is your chance to check out the cool MC12 up close!

A True-Blue Interior

The clean, blue interior of the MC12 is packed with awesome accessories and a daring dashboard. Ultra-cool instruments, which include an oval clock and a blue engine-start button, are located on a titanium-colored console. This stylized tunnel also includes a storage compartment and a 12-volt outlet. A central speedometer is placed right in front of the driver. The upper part of the leather and carbon-trimmed steering wheel is slightly flattened, and the super-sweet seats are upholstered in fabric. The doors have carbon-fiber panels and pockets complete with electric window buttons. The pedals are aluminum and the mats rubber. Inside, this car is one rockin' ride!

Slender, Sleek, and Smooth

This two-seater has a removable hard top, turning the MC12 into a convertible in seconds flat. It has a long wheelbase (110.2 inches), and is made of a high-tech mixture of metals. This helps keep the car light, which is key in allowing ultra-fast speed. Above the hard top, there is a snorkellike tunnel that extends to the engine compartment in the rear. The MC12's bodywork is made entirely of carbon fiber, as is its chassis. This helps absorb bumps, and also guarantees an excellent standard of safety for even the fastest daredevil drivers.

Radical Rear Section

The back of the MC12 is dominated by two things: its 6.0-liter, 630-horsepower V-12 engine, and a slender wing with two fins. At the car's base lies a small spoiler in which a third stoplight has been placed. The inverted half-moon design of the exhausts is the most striking part of the tail section. The MC12 delivers a maximum 652 lb-ft of torque and remains exceptionally graceful while charging around the track.

FAST FACTS

Origin:	**Italy**
Top speed:	**205 mph**
Engine:	**6.0-liter V-12, 630hp**
Length:	**202.5 inches**
Width:	**82.5 inches**
Base price:	**$500,000 (estimated)**

MERCEDES MAYBACH 62
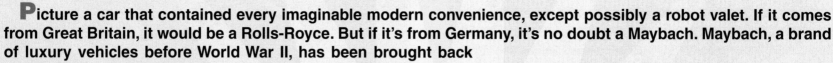

Picture a car that contained every imaginable modern convenience, except possibly a robot valet. If it comes from Great Britain, it would be a Rolls-Royce. But if it's from Germany, it's no doubt a Maybach. Maybach, a brand of luxury vehicles before World War II, has been brought back to life by Mercedes-Benz to capture some of the Rolls customers. Personally crafted, Maybachs come in two forms: the shorter, sportier Maybach 57; and the ultra-luxurious, long-wheelbase Maybach 62 (pictured here).

Backseat Hideout

The Maybach 62 is less like a car and more like a limousine. The huge backseat is so big, there are buttons on the door frames so passengers won't have to stretch to close them. The doors power close at the flick of a switch. Curtains in the back keep the interior private. The standard DVD player and twin monitors, TV tuner, CD changer, and 21-speaker Dolby/Bose sound system are entertainment enough, but a passenger can also bring an MP3 player or a PlayStation 2 and plug it in. Wireless headphones allow each rear passenger and the driver up front to listen to or play with what they please.

Speeding

Maybach drivers will find more than enough power with this car's 543-horsepower, twin-turbocharged V-12 engine with 664 lb-ft of torque. Mated to a 5-speed automatic transmission, the Maybach 62 will accelerate from 0 to 60 mph in about 5.4 seconds and run up to 155 mp. This car also sports all the safety equipment you can imagine, including 10 airbags, 2 of them shielding rear occupants from the side glass in case of an accident. If that happens, the standard Tele Aid system will automatically notify the police.

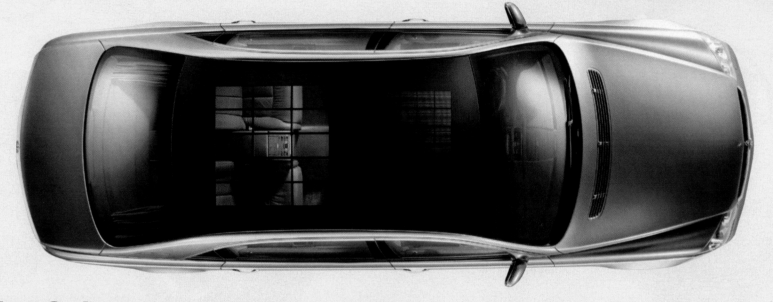

Taking Orders

When you're buying a $359,500 car built to order, half the fun is going through the process of picking out every little detail, from the size of the sunroof to the type of game system to go in the back—Nintendo, Sega, Sony, or maybe all three! Maybach takes the buying process just as seriously as its customers. To order a Maybach, buyers visit a center where they can choose from a range of leather, wood, and other trims, or they can take their own materials and paint colors and have Maybach use those. It takes four to six months to build the custom car from that point. While buyers are waiting, Maybach invites them on special trips: skiing weekends or exotic vacations. Finally, the car arrives in its own container, from the home port in Germany, to the buyer's door. Now that's ultra cool service!

FAST FACTS

Origin:	Germany
Top speed:	155 mph
Engine:	5.5-liter twin-turbo charged V-12, 543 hp
Length:	242.5 inches
Width:	78.0 inches
Base price:	$359,500

BUICK VELITE

Buick has a 100-year-old reputation for elegant, refined style. But it has been a few decades since they had a four-seat convertible to call its own. Now Buick has a concept car that is a future fast four-seat ragtop. It's called the Velite—named for a special group of fast-moving soldiers in Napoleon's army. Built to be rich, elegant, and speedy, the Velite concept was designed by Buick and built at the world-famous Bertone studios in Italy. It blends classic American style with modern, high-performance hardware like nothing else that has come from America in decades.

Back to the Future

Buick's classic cars were rear-wheel drive, and the Velite returns the brand to that winning formula. The Velite's athletic proportions and aggressive stance show off its bold, modern design. The cockpit, set back behind a long hood, is perched on 20-inch front wheels with short overhangs, giving the Velite a sleek, sporty profile.

The Velite's long, sculpted clamshell hood spotlights a new waterfall grille with a jewel-like finish. The hood integrates portholes—three per side—in a nod to Buick's past, while the hood tilts forward when opened, like the brand's classic cars. The crystalline head-lamps use new X-Beam technology, with smaller lenses and higher intensity for a more focused light pattern. The taillamps are X-Beams too, with cooling vents.

Techno Beat

Power to move the Velite comes from Buick's twin-turbocharged, intercooled global V-6 engine. Right now, it's a concept engine, but it's sure to make its home in future Buicks. It has 400 horse-power and 400 lb-ft of torque, thanks to a high-tech double-overhead cam design and 3.6 liters of displacement. The engine sports variable valve-timing technology, which helps it get better fuel economy and performance. The exhaust flows out of the engine through a pair of large oval-shaped exhaust outlets. The V-6 is coupled to a Hydra-Matic 6L80-E 6-speed, rear-wheel-drive automatic transmission that is equipped with manual tap-shift gear selection.

Luxury Liner

The Velite's interior puts the most luxurious finishes together with all the standard equipment that an ultra cool four-seater would need. Buick aimed for a jazz-club interior with cool lighting—the gentle glow of the cabin's lights are color-matched with the gold-leaf trim that replaces the usual wood and leather seating. The center console includes XM satellite radio, as well as OnStar emergency services, which notify the police if the car is in an accident. The "E-lock" security system allows the Velite's driver to lock or unlock the vehicle without fumbling for a key. The system uses a special signal that allows for starting and driving without a regular ignition key.

FAST FACTS	
Origin:	USA
Top speed:	186 mph
Engine:	3.6-liter twin-turbo V-6, 450 hp
Length:	186.0 inches
Width:	75.6 inches
Base price:	$50,000 (estimated)

BMW 645Ci

BMW builds ultimate driving machines, from the hot Z4 roadster to the slinky 7-Series sedan. Now BMW is returning to the classic "grand touring" market with the 645Ci, a convertible (and a coupe, too) that combines swanky style, a big V-8 motor, rear-wheel drive, and exceptional handling in one stunning shape. With its sweeping and graceful design, quick-acting convertible top, and effortless speed from its 8-cylinder engine, this 645Ci is the best BMW for boulevard cruising.

In the Hot Seat

The 645Ci's interior is sporty and stylish. BMW offers the choice of wood or aluminum trim. There's a big controller called iDrive that operates all the A/C and audio settings. Along with the leather trim, there are dual-zone digital climate controls; power seats; windows and doors; rain-sensing wipers; and a kickin' Harman Kardon premium audio system with CD changer.

Speed Demon

The 645Ci looks elegant, but underneath the hood is a raging 325-horsepower V-8 that rockets the convertible to 60 mph in about 6 seconds. Better yet, the engine can make noise like the biggest, baddest muscle cars of the 1960s. At cruising speed, the V-8 gives off a soft purr, but at full throttle, it turns into a massive roar.

The powerful power plant comes with a choice of three different transmissions: a 6-speed stick, a 6-speed automatic, or a 6-speed sequential manual gearbox (SMG). The 6-speed is a slick throw from gear to gear, the automatic is responsive and easy to drive, and the SMG is an electronically shifted manual transmission like the ones used in Formula One racing.

A true grand tourer, the 645Ci is a smooth ride. And the steering is sweet, too—like a laser guiding this ultra cool car from curve to curve.

Hardtop or Sunshine

With BMW's big two-door, a driver can have it either way—as a sleek, hardtop coupe or a hot, Hollywood-style ragtop. No matter which style a driver picks, the 645Ci is packed with the kind of technology that sounds like it might be found on a space shuttle. There is active roll stabilization, a feature that adjusts the car's suspension speciifically for the condition of the road; "adaptive" xenon headlights, which can swivel to help light up curving roadways; active steering, which changes the amount of power assist based on how fast the 645Ci is going; and a head-up display (HUD) that projects data such as vehicle speed and turn-by-turn navigation guidance onto a mirrored portion of the windshield. It's totally high-tech!

Origin:	**Germany**
Top speed:	**155 mph**
Engine:	**4.4-liter V-8, 325 hp**
Length:	**190.0 inches**
Width:	**73.0 inches**
Base price:	**$76,995**

ASTON MARTIN DB9

Aston Martin is one of the longest-lived names in sports-car history. Now a part of the Ford Motor Company, Aston Martin is bringing in a whole new generation of sports-car excitement for car enthusiasts and James Bond fans alike. Case in point: the DB9—a raging 2+2 machine with staggering V-12 power, a stunningly handsome body, and an ultra-rich interior. It is timeless, totally modern, and can stomp out 60-mph runs in fewer than 5 seconds. And because it's mostly hand-built, Aston owners can personalize their very own supercars.

Space-Age Construction

The Aston Martin DB9's body is truly remarkable. Though it looks like Aston's past—the classic DB4 and DB5s are some of its direct influences—it is built unlike any other modern automobile. Its aluminum body is constructed in sections, then fastened together. The space-age construction makes it tighter, stronger, and lighter than any of its supercar competitors. It also allows the body to fit together with fewer lines, making the DB9 look like it was cut from a single piece of metal.

The DB9 weighs only about 3,700 lb, which is extraordinary for a V-12 sports car capable of 186 mph. But Aston Martin uses other tricks to make the DB9 fast and furious. The gearbox is located in the rear of the car, which helps give the car the perfect weight balance for great handling.

The aluminum suspension puts less weight on the wheels, leading to quicker and more precise steering. And Aston uses carbon fiber for the driveshaft—the connection between the engine and the rear wheels—for strength and lightweight performance.

Techno Beat

The high-tech race doesn't end with the DB9's body or its massively powerful 6.0-liter V-12. Its transmission is a 6-speed automatic outfitted with drive-by-wire controls that use computers to tell the engine and transmission how to work together. The transmission also can be shifted manually by paddles mounted behind the steering wheel. A regular 6-speed manual gearbox will be offered as well.

To go along with the advanced gearboxes, the DB9 comes with tons of safety equipment. Stability control will keep even the worst driver out of serious trouble by using the antilock brakes to slow the car if it skids in a corner. Plenty of airbags protect passengers in case of an accident.

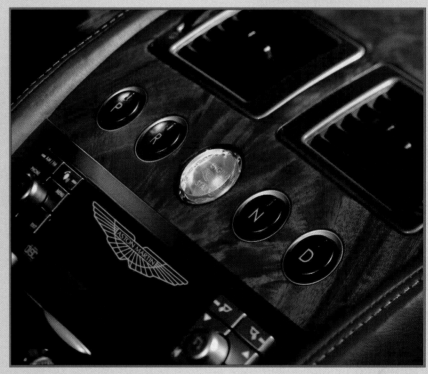

Interior

The DB9's cockpit can wear whatever the driver wants—whether it's classic wood or bamboo trim with leather and chrome. More-modern aluminum trim can be specified, as well as any paint color the owner wants. British sound-system experts are in charge of the megawatt audio system. The Aston Martin logo glows gloriously on a screen located in the console. Leave it to the British to make a classy interior that is equal parts supercar and super-luxury.

FAST FACTS

Origin:	**Great Britain**
Top speed:	**186 mph**
Engine:	**6.0-liter V-12, 450 hp**
Length:	**184.9 inches**
Width:	**73.8 inches**
Base price:	**$155,000 coupe; $165,000 Volante convertible**

CADILLAC ESCALADE ESV

Cadillac is the newest star of the hip-hop scene. This massive SUV, designed for luxury-minded customers, has also found a whole new set of fans in rich young celebs who want to cruise cool behind this car's knife-edged style. The Escalade gets all up in your grille with its grille—and behind the power of a hulking V-8, it's the most capable luxury SUV anywhere.

Big, Bold, and Brawny

The Escalade ESV is the roomiest, most powerful full-size luxury SUV available. It's 22 inches longer than the standard Escalade, with more than 20 extra inches of interior room. This means bigger and better seating, and even more room to stash your gold records in back.

Outside, it's all flash, with the same snappy, edgy lines found on the regular Escalade. The massive front end commands attention, especially behind the clock-sized Cadillac wreath and crest badge. High-intensity headlamps with chrome bezels light up the front end (and everything in a 100-foot path), making the ESV an excellent car to drive, no matter what the weather.

The ESV's hugely powerful power plant sends this truck into orbit as quickly as some sports cars. The Vortec H.O. 6,000 V-8 engine cranks out 345 horsepower at 5,200 rpm and 380 lb-ft of torque at 4,000 rpm. That's enough to tow 7,700 lb, or a two-horse trailer. The transmission is a 4-speed, electronically controlled automatic that's beefed up for the heavy-duty road work that Cadillac drivers put the ESV through.

For all-weather capability, the Escalade ESV sports a standard, full-time, all-wheel-drive (AWD) system. It automatically and continuously transfers power to the wheels without a hint that it's working—other than its improved grip, that is. The system is linked directly to an antispin system, and antilock brakes ensure that drivers stay safe, even if weather the conditions are poor.

Fully Stocked

Name a piece of high-tech gear available on today's cars and trucks, and it's standard on the Escalade ESV. In addition to all-wheel drive (AWD) and StabiliTrak with road-sensing suspension (RSS), the ESV adds ultrasonic rear parking assist (no more rear-end collisions), OnStar, XM satellite radio, a premium Bose sound system, and a Bvlgari-designed analog clock. Plus, it has an available rear seat DVD system and a DVD-based navigation system that provides turn-by-turn directions to thousands of points of interest. The back has a slick sunroof and is fitted with some of the most comfortable seats ever to go into a heavy-duty truck. Luscious leather covers the seats on the first and second seat rows, with more durable leather on the third-row bench.

The front bucket seats have 10-way-power cushion adjusters, power-adjustable side bolsters and power lumbar, power seat-back recliners, and heated seatbacks and cushions with three separate settings. For the biggest amount of interior room in its class, the Escalade's second- and third-row seatbacks fold flat, creating a huge cargo area with a flat load surface. There's no denying that this is one ultra-comfy ride!

FAST FACTS

Origin:	USA
Top speed:	125 mph
Engine:	6.0-liter V-8, 345 hp
Length:	184.9 inches
Width:	73.8 inches
Base price:	$60,000

FORD MUSTANG GT

It has been more than 20 years since a brand-new Mustang has rolled off the line, but the time has come! Heading down from Dearborn, Michigan, is the Ford Mustang GT. It is the first renovation of the classic pony car since 1979, and easily one of the best-looking efforts to come from Ford's design studios since the 1990s. With all-new mechanicals underneath the skin, such as rear-wheel drive and a live-axle chassis (powered by the driver's choice of a V-6 or a V-8 engine), the Mustang is back and better than ever!

Motor Magic

The 4.6-liter, 60-degree V-8 replaces the 3.8-liter 90-degree engine found in previous models. It also bests the old engine's output by a horsepower of 7. A manual 5-speed gearbox is included, but a 5-speed automatic is optional. The 4.6-liter V-8 is the motorhead's best friend. Three-valve heads help it breathe better, even while running on regular unleaded. Electronic throttle control and a variable camshaft have been introduced with the upgraded engine.

Past, Present, and Future

The shape of this Mustang is like the greatest hit of all Mustangs. "We weren't just redesigning a car, we were adding another chapter to an epic," says J. Mays, Ford Motor Company's group vice president of design. The long-deck, short-rear silhouette of every Mustang in history returns with a new shape, and it's far more authentic-looking than past models. Three-piece taillamps, *C*-shaped side scoops, circular headlights, and a forward-angled nose establish the cool character of this 'Stang.

Old-School Interior

The interior shows Ford's pride in its history. This Mustang contains hints of the famous car's past, but it certainly isn't stuck in the 1960s. Chrome gauge rings and aluminum panels dress it up in the finest retro style. A six-inch increase in wheelbase makes a backseat that passengers can actually fit in comfortably—something missing in past 'Stangs. Among the standard features are one-touch up/down power windows, power mirrors, keyless entry and power locks, a heated rear window, and interval wipers. Sound systems include a standard CD player and an optional 1,000-watt Shaker Audiophile system.

FAST FACTS

Origin:	USA
Top speed:	140 mph
Engine:	4.6-liter V-8, 450 hp
Length:	187.6 inches
Width:	72.1 inches
Base price:	$20,000 - $25,000

CHRYSLER PT CRUISER CONVERTIBLE

Chrysler is the company for sun and fun, with the widest range of convertibles available in America. The PT Cruiser convertible may look like a blast from the past, but this baby is all new. Cool lines, breezy ragtop capability, and all the modern equipment that you would expect from these convertible experts are right here. But what makes this car super cool is its size. The PT convertible has plenty of room for four people and their beach gear. It also has the available power to blister the pavement.

Top-Down Fun

Chrysler made certain that the convertible-ization of the PT Cruiser didn't ruffle the retro's excellent road manners. To keep the cruiser's handling intact, Chrysler installed a color-keyed sport bar made of hydroformed steel, which connects the rear quarter panels for rock-steady road holding. Two flush-mounted lamps light the rear seats, and the bar itself cuts down on the amount of wind blowing in on rear-seat riders. The convertible top is a top-drawer effort, too. The three-layer cloth top has a glass heated rear window, and comes in black or taupe. The top feels soft to the touch, and makes the cabin as soundproof as any convertible offered by the company. It's easy to use, too: All you do is release the two latches using a single D-shaped handle on the windshield header, then push the top's power button on the center stack. The top has a cover that snaps on when the top is lowered for a clean, tight look.

Retro Cool

What makes Chrysler's PT Cruiser so cool is its retro style—and it looks even better as a hot-rodded convertible. The grille is classic Chrysler from the 1930s, with cycle-style fenders and a lowered stance. Teardrop head-lamps and taillamps finish off the retro look outside.

Something for Everyone

The PT Cruiser convertible comes in three trim levels, each with its own version of Chrysler's 2.4-liter DOHC 16-valve 4-cylinder engine. The Standard starts at $19,995 and comes with 15-inch steel wheels and a 150-horsepower, 2.4-liter engine. The mid-range Touring model adds turbocharging to the 4-cylinder engine for 180 horsepower and shifts through a 4-speed automatic. Sixteen-inch, 7-spoke, painted cast aluminum wheels come standard; 6-spoke, chrome finish aluminum 16s are optional, as are antilock brakes. The top of the line is the $28,155 PT Cruiser convertible GT (the car featured here): It gets a high-output, 200-horsepower 2.4-liter 4-cylinder engine with either a 5-speed manual or a 4-speed automatic with semi-manual autostick control. To that, add standard antilock brakes, a sport-tuned suspension, 17-inch wheels, leather seats, and a leather-wrapped steering wheel.

Room to Roam

Passengers can fit in the PT Cruiser convertible and won't complain about second-class accommodations in the back. With 84.3 cubic feet of space, this PT offers up more rear-seat and cargo room than most four-seat convertibles, and nearly 10 inches more rear leg room than any competitor. Nine different seat configurations, and a pass-through trunk opening with enough room to store two golf bags, make this car way more useful than most ragtops.

The cool cockpit complements the car's exterior. The body color comes into play on the dash panels, the manual shifter gets a long lever and a ball top like the hottest street rods from the 1950s, and the gauges have a cool retro flair. This PT convertible was made for ultra-cool cruising.

FAST FACTS

Origin:	**USA**
Top speed:	**130 mph**
Engine:	**2.4-liter turbcharged in-line four, 200 hp**
Length:	**168.8 inches**
Width:	**67.1 inches**
Base price:	**$19,995-$28,155**

The recipe is a good one: Take a world-class sport sedan and wedge in the biggest engine that will fit. Cadillac has done it before, but never in a car the size of its new CTS-V, a 400-horsepower answer to BMW's best M3 sports sedans. With endless power and torque, a great manual gearbox, and handling straight off the toughest racetrack in the world, the CTS-V is a clear sign that the best-handling cars in the world don't just come from Europe. Cadillac has regained its former role as one of the world's best luxury car builders.

Motor Madness

When Cadillac's engineers first designed the CTS-V, they didn't think that there would be room for a big V-8 engine under the hood. But after studying it, they figured out that the Corvette V-8 would slip in easily and without major changes to the CTS-V's front end. The massive engine generates 400 horsepower, the same as the Corvette C6 (see p. 9), and twists out an amazing 395 lb-ft of torque. The engine churns out all that power thanks to a new induction system that brings more air into the engine's cylinders and gives it a growling howl at high speed. The CTS-V's amazing power kicks it to 60 mph in 4.6 seconds, on its way to a top speed of 163 mph.

Art and Science

The edgy style of the CTS-V is part of Cadillac's art-and-science theme, which replaces the soft round shapes of the past with crisp edges and bold lines. The chassis is stiff and robust—so tight, it only needed a crossbrace over the massive engine, and a thicker cradle for its rear axle. Outside, you can tell the CTS-V from the slower CTS by its V-Series badge on the left side of the trunk, and the bright chrome mesh that replaces the base car's egg-crate grille. For braking, there are four-piston front Brembo brakes, and big rear brakes. The retuned CTS-V suspension has springs that are 27 percent stiffer for tighter handling, and the tires are upgraded to high-performance Goodyear Eagle F1 245/45 run-flats.

Stuffed With Stuff

The CTS-V brings earth-shattering performance to the game, with a price tag that is lower than a lot of hot European cars. To go with the price tag, there's a navigation system and great new sport seats with power lumbar controls, as well as a power passenger seat. There's also a new set of white-on-black gauges, and a computer that tells a driver how well he or she can tackle corners. Plenty of equipment and trim are on the standard list, including dual front airbags, side airbags for the front seat, seat-belt pretensioners, antilock brakes, traction control, and electronic stability control with competition mode. There's also dual-zone climate control, power driver and front-passenger seats, steering-wheel-mounted audio and cruise controls, multifunction CD/AM/FM audio system, and fog lamps. That's a lot of awesome stuff stuffed into one ultra cool car!

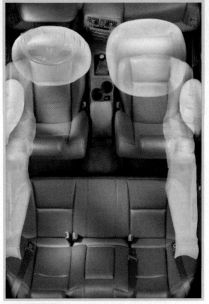

FAST FACTS	
Origin:	USA
Top speed:	163 mph
Engine:	5.7-liter V-8, 400 hp
Length:	191.5 inches
Width:	70.6 inches
Base price:	$49,995

PONTIAC GTO

American muscle cars are the stuff of legend. Pontiac had the muscle car that defined the era: the massively powerful GTO. By 1974, fuel-economy regulations put the GTO back into the garage. But technology is a great thing, particularly for cars. Computers have allowed vehicles to become more powerful and more fuel-efficient at the same time. This has brought back some great names, including the GTO. Pontiac has gone around the world to recreate its famous hot rod, eventually plucking a two-door coupe from Australia and jamming a big Corvette motor under its hood. Rock and roll is back, and it's in the shape of this two-door Pontiac GTO.

Rockin' and Rollin'

The GTO contains some excellent inner hardware from Australia. The steering, with its sharp reflexes, makes ordinary drivers drive better. The big brakes automatically haul the massive coupe down from illegal speeds; and the suspension feels just like the muscle cars of the past. With 17-inch 245/45ZR tires and smart-looking 5-spoke wheels, it's grippy, comfortable, and safe for all.

Hot Looks Inside and Out

The sleek shape of the GTO looks grown-up and powerful, like the original GTO. Inside the cabin are NASA-style red gauges that match the exterior color, and awesome aluminum trim. Air-conditioning, a power driver's seat, cruise control, an AM/FM CD sound system, and 17-inch alloy wheels are all standard on this Aussie import.

Corvette Soul

The GTO's 5.7-liter V-8 rumbles and roars like nothing else. With 350 horsepower at 5,200 rpm, and 365 lb-ft of torque at 4,000 rpm, nearly any gear in the standard 6-speed manual will blast drivers ahead of other sports cars on the highway. That holds true for either the manual 6-speed gearbox or the 4-speed automatic. Pontiac says that the GTO will accelerate to 60 mph in 5.3 seconds in manual-equipped versions. The manual will run through the quarter-mile in 13.8 seconds at 105 mph, in the same time but 3 mph faster than the automatic. Short of a Corvette, General Motors can't offer you much else that's faster, sleeker, or V-8 powered.

Origin:	USA/Australia
Top speed:	150 mph
Engine:	5.7-liter V-8, 350 hp
Length:	189.8 inches
Width:	72.5 inches
Base price:	$33,190

NISSAN 350Z ROADSTER

Nissan calls it the heart of its brand—the classic Z sports car. From its first edition in the early 1970s, through the spectacular 300ZX grand tourers of the 1990s, to the sharp-edged 350Z sports car of today, it's easy to see why Nissan considers this car the very best it has to offer. But what's left to give to drivers with a big wallet and a need for speed? How about a 150-mph convertible with good looks, an easy-to-use converttop, and a sticker price below $35,000? That's what the 350Z Roadster (often called the Z) is all about.

Firmly in Charge

The Z Roadster shares the same FM (front midship) platform as the 350Z coupe. To beef it up for the convertible surgery, Nissan added reinforcements to the floor in the shape of a big *V*, and an *A*-shaped bar across the front end. Reinforcing bars were also added across the door openings and behind the seats.

The Z Roadster kicks out a massive 287 horsepower from its 3.5-liter V-6 engine shared with the 350Z coupe. With 274 lb-ft of torque and variable valve timing, the engine is a growling, howling success. There's plenty of power all across the rev range. The engine mates up to either a 6-speed close-ratio manual or a 5-speed automatic transmission.

The Z Roadster shares the wedgy attitude of the 350Z coupe and cranks it up a notch or two. The instrument panel features three big gauge pods. The center stack can be outfitted with an optional navigation system with a 7-inch display. Details like metallic door vents and center console trim give the car a high-tech edge. The regular seats are tailored for performance driving, but optional ventilated leather seats are another way to go. Upholstered in hot burnt-orange leather, they come with a woven center section and have an opening in the seat back for better wind flow and ventilation.

Ragin' Ragtop

A winning convertible needs a sharp profile and an easy-to-use convertible top—and that's what the Z Roadster brings to the game. The Z Roadster's fully automatic soft top lowers in 20 seconds and offers up a heated-glass rear window and a lightweight powered cover that completely hides the top when down. It's easy to lower it, too. All you do is push the brake pedal and hold the button (located to the left of the steering column), and the top opens or closes automatically. To keep turbulence in the two-seater to a minimum, a glass wind deflector between the seats makes sure the wind moves out and over the cabin.

The Roadster model has power seats, power-operated soft top, rear wind deflector, 17-inch alloy wheels, xenon headlights, automatic climate control, and a choice of transmissions. The Touring model adds a Bose audio system with a 6-disc CD changer and 7 speakers, plus leather-appointed seats with heater and heated mirrors. The Roadster comes with just about everything a driver needs to be happy—except maybe continuous sunshine.

FAST FACTS

Origin:	Japan
Top speed:	150 mph
Engine:	3.5-liter V-6, 450 hp
Length:	169.4 inches
Width:	71.5 inches
Base price:	$34,610

VW CONCEPT C

This exciting concept car provides a view of things to come from Volkswagen. What makes this automobile so unique—and awesome—is its design. The future-forward look of VW's Concept C, with its slick metallic finish and sleek interior style, takes this ride to a whole new level. The same is true of its technology: The Concept C features a ton of newly developed high-tech gadgets that would make any driver drool. Not to mention that the Concept C is basically two vehicles in one, indicated by the *C*, which stands for both coupe (a two-door, enclosed car) and cabriolet (a two-door convertible).

Easy-Going Interior

The dual-tone interior of the VW Concept C is as attractive as its exterior. The dashboard and instrument panel have a rich green color, while a lighter beige tone has been given to the seats, upholstery, and all interior elements below the window rails. The inner section of the seats is made especially stylish by the contrasting stripes running across them. The newly developed cockpit, with its instruments set in brushed aluminium frames, gives this car its sporty character.

A Dream Design

The Concept C's unique style includes the distinctive quadrilateral headlamps with rounded base sections, a deep arrow-shaped grille (made from aluminum), and sleek rear lights. The slight slant of the hood over the headlamps creates the impression of eyebrows.

Hood Happenings

One thing about the Concept C that makes it ultra cool is its folding steel roof. This four-seat VW can transform from a coupe to a cabriolet in a matter of seconds with the press of a button. The new, 5-level, electrohydraulic hardtop system in the Concept C is a multitalented, trifunctional solution: a coupe roof, a sliding sunroof, and a cabriolet roof all incorporated into the one system. This type of combination, in this form, is unique and special, making for one truly radical ride!

VW Power

The Concept C is driven by a 110-kW, 150-horsepower FSI engine. It's a 6-speed manual gearbox, and can go from zero to 60 in no-time flat. (Though VW won't yet give the exact number away!) Don't let its distinguished exterior fool you—this car has performance power that will get any car lover fully enthused!

FAST FACTS

Origin:	Germany
Top speed:	130 mph (estimated)
Engine:	110-kW, 150-hp FSI
Length:	173.6 inches
Width:	71.3 inches
Base price:	$30,000